DATE DUE			

OTHER BOOKS

Poetry
A Fall Journal
My Grandfather's Pants
Carmela Bianca
Bird As
Avis
Species of Intoxication
Just Like a Real Italian Kid
Continental Harmony
gyptian in hortulus
Interferon
No Both
Too Much Johnson
cured in the going bebop

Collaboration
Lowell Connector (with Clark Coolidge & John Yau)
Rejection (with Trevor Winkfield & Geoffrey Young)

Spoken Word
cured in the going bebop

MICHAEL GIZZI

MY TERZA RIMA

THE FIGURES

2001

Cover photograph by Tim Davis, 2000
Page six image: "Zweiter Schnabelkopf"
by Franz Xaver Messerschmidt (1736-1783)
Author photograph by Elena Dovydenas

Grateful acknowledgement to the editors of the various periodicals
in which some of these poems first appeared: *Shiny, Lungfull, The
Germ, The Hat, DC Poetry, Bombay Gin, Combo, Faucheuse, The
Baffler, Skanky Possum, The East Village, Jacket, New American
Writing,* and *The Blind See Only This World : Poems for John
Wieners* (Granary Books/Pressed Wafer, 2000).

Too Much Johnson first appeared as a chapbook from The Figures
(on the author's fiftieth birthday, 1999); *cured in the going bebop*
(with cover by Ippy Patterson) appeared in 2000 from Paradigm
Press. Utopia Productions brought out a CD of the poet reading
cured in the going bebop (with cover collage by Barbieo Barros
Gizzi), 2000.

The publisher wishes to thank the Saul Rosen Foundation
for its continued and generous support.

The Figures, 5 Castle Hill Ave., Gt. Barrington, MA 01230
Distributed by Small Press Distribution, Berkeley, CA

for my mother

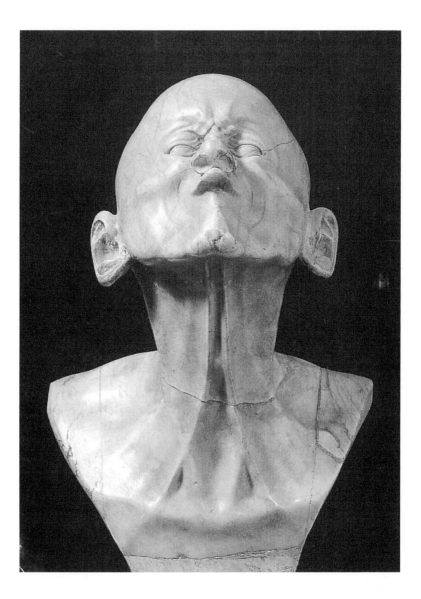

1. MY TERZA RIMA

2. CURED IN THE GOING BEBOP

3. TOO MUCH JOHNSON

MY TERZA RIMA

to Providence

"We had locked the Tongue
in the basement,
where we were afraid to go..."

Ray Ragosta

I. *A SWEEPING LOOK AT HARD CANDY*

Imagine you're a myopic tree hugger
   permanently attached to the buttocks
   of a limousine like the one in Moby Dick

a big frontal flop lays down its pancake
   orphan all future fly goo
   shake mothballs from bric-a-brac

wolf spigots awake pink-bottomed evening
   emerges from the trampoline
   if you'll pardon the extrusions

this is the scenery nearly supreme
   glucose cavalries in gel-capped regiments
   pates among O'Sheas

oremus for us photogenic
   enough to vanish
   into dust

II. *A TREATISE ON COWLICKS*

If you don't know what you want
   try bigamy try RFD Hopalong Cassidy
   go in and out the window

Malevich in mufti studies husbandry
   rehearsing superimpositions
   "I used to do a pretty good ocean"

under the weather shooting stars whiz in our hats
   so the brandy bottle's poetry
   a nod to British physics

and the big fist of bran
   when we do chestnuts like Pip
   or six feet away upstage

propinquity one
   has to leave word to have it
   and you've had it

III. *ADVENTURES IN POULTRY*

"Chicken" Khachaturian cuts quite
   a figure like Buddha but
   only the belly

Get thee to a bocci ball and
   ask for Pepto Miseri
   download your prunes

the sky is falling and
   its noms de plumes
   like steam rising from

Skeezix the primordial
   just sorta comes back
   a renegade hugging gumbo

or is it alien sap atomic pablum
   to rub on the phone so lying
   spreads the clap

how all occasions do vet
   his confidence now Bartleby
   now a bantam forward and back

IV.   *AGENT GINKGO VIAGRA*

What if polka dots are Polish moondrops?
   we be zen when we can
   Spermaceti, draw me

a White Whale on tap pour it
   in this ostrich baron's looking glass
   now stir in sixteen houris

equivalent to the longitude
   cordoned off by astronomical
   silk slips at high altitude

one hundred rainy day puzzles
   pour sugar on the prisoner of thin air
   like kooky Kwakiutl risotto

let my beanie go retard
   let midnight measure the land
   today I met Temptation

in her holster a Shanghai lamb
   my yen
   the finest Asian stem

V.   *AN UNDENIABLE QUIVERING IN THE LATITUDES*

A bee's affections prestidigitation
   imperial dog flips fifty flags above
   zest and parade bottle caps

waving deposit tell their story
   to a spittoon "Heck
   I spent Rockefeller's pet dime"

and moonlighting as a mattress
   clouds pass by almost aluminum
   as into every life there comes a logging

company and a 300 pound Pine Sol means
   to make of you pâté what's wrong
   is right as rain its offspring

almost shocking to look up from come
   in the form of flashbacks while over-eating
   a point on the ceiling to

see that moment the big hand
   get to less while the clock plays
   the song of what to look at next

so drab it must be startled
   every time its inflation
   marvels out of nowhere

VI.   *BLEEDER'S IMPROMPTU*

Heart inside punching bag
   hearing and braille
   stacked on an egg

fructified by the smitten groove
   hitch your muffin to a hackberry
   this month's all american kraut

pulls out a plum glass blowers
   are chock full o' sand and
   if you stretch your name brand

chums the free range rolls seem stingy
   so one never knows what
   to expect from whipped potatoes

know why oyster shootists march in sync?
   class infatuation Sousa
   flirting with whole cream

can't stop canoodling
   the immutables will soon be
   landing a vision shows up in his ear

the jamoke jubilato
   baroque window blues
   are here

VII.   *BOP WESTERN*

"Doc" Scurlock trolls
   the Hematomas for simonized
   crooners and Black Bings

Botticellis that make ears
   owls in a molecule of italic
   Nature Boy listens in longhand

to the muttering under his vest during
   the needle jump jig
   like beard hairs on a death mask

there'll come a day bar lines
   can't negotiate "Tumblin' Tumbleweed"
   but Quimo Sabe'll grease the skids

with a rhyming dictionary
   scalping Brother Dexter
   a long drink of rhythm his "Kong

Neptune" turning somersaults
   above the abyss (that's why they
   call it life) forget the bridge

to "Wagon Wheels" best masticate
   with hymnists or watch a sideman
   kick the smile off your face

VIII.   *BOTCHER'S PARADISE*

Avast ye boogers of breast-beating!
  gassing on about
  Vinegar Hill Hoopsar

sufferin' sciatica have ya
  had this tooth pulled before
  if so

subtract all hostlers isolatos
  and oolong fillies from
  your planetary stable

and you'll have a very small
  wolfhound salaaming dogma
  tune in next week for Heroes

of Butter zombie momzers
  from the Halls of Montezuma
  devoted to head spin and

cognitive beer if such a description
  isn't oxymoronic sequestered in
  dithery privy to the phone poles

of the Milky Way back before
  aromatherapy turned
  taxidermy into VJ Day

IX.   *BUCKLE DOWN BELCHERTOWN*

I only have eyes for
   you and all the things you think
   one nation underwater adjacent

the church unavoidable as Lulu
   and the Dogstar my dog has perfect
   pitch and can read the paper

before it hits the porch
   a myocardial mutt racing full pelt
   to a home-cooked mess without the meal

clobber 'em on the cruller!
   it's too humid for Bruckner
   shit upsets my liver

you'll form new attachments you'll die last
   some even die grateful
   crapulous in a hackney Woonsocket

what're you gonna do
   about it—"Tea for Two"?
   your father's moustache and Dave's

missing adipose smoke Herbert
   Tareyton beneath a North Atlantic tree
   baseballs begin to weep

X. *BURNT END OF A GARDENER*

Dexterity's bunchflowers
   torture both sides of the fence
   with an income of roses

dead in a failed snapshot
   two milliseconds into a fairy tale
   flies on real tapestry

I thought I'd go a mite
   dizzy marooned in moleskin
   a goumba Johnny

discussing peg legs with enough booty beadwork
   to disappear at sea
   Yo-ho-ho

nautical rum made me
   nondenominational looks like
   the drip feed from the stateroom's invading

the tulips too including
   what little firmament
   I could fit into this lullaby

XI.   *COOKOUT AT SYRINGA RANCH*

Cracks appear in fluid engineering
    Hephaestus prepares to void
    quiver my veils but the other side of

ambergris is like coming on the Hudson
    in the evening to excavate the threadbare
    a great person in one sandwich

whose heat is the result of gingersnaps
    sent to beach the stars and a very big cheese
    was Rumford who later wrote

a villanelle called "Menageries
    of the Magnificent Countertop"
    minting donut bombs for cosmonauts

while seniors make water
    chiefly by proxy all
    in a day's lumbago

XII.   *GONE BAMBOO*

Spent Saint Full-of-Hisself
　　had been a Beechnut Baby
　　we were in Waco to interview his Evinrude

his liquid decimal system
　　made me wonder about dimples
　　if fish gotta fly birds have to

voîlà what needn't happen
　　is an Alsatian one man band
　　going pond pedestrian

halt all pensée of such a critter
　　your average bubble is actually
　　a sailor's navel

if a lion could talk he'd say
　　he needs to drop near 300 stone
　　to march on the sea

any messiah's too puny
　　when the spider
　　drives the shoe

XIII.   *HAM ON A RAINBOW*

A big ole peony pops me in the roseola
   to convolute your population
   pollinate a posy

piss write in the dust
   mumble and be amazed
   igloo moon wearing nothing but sky

has the dry heaves
   Mexico Chablis
   money isn't everything if you count clouds

if I had all night I'd be
   an inflight rainy day davenport
   stacked with alexandrines

parthenogenesists make marionettes
   Cheeky Rodriquez uses magnets
   from epilepsy to aerial-rigging

ethereal pinups say it best
   "seen any snaggleteeth
   come through here yet?"

and true as rubber cement
   in the wind from the men's room
   herdboys make a breakthrough

"let's not do anything
   on the 'lower 48'
   general issue's bad feng shui"

XIV. *IN THE NAMEWAKES*

Ur Popeye out of stir sub rosa
   with Liquid Santa windswept and
   by nothing less than the ionosphere

like Ben Bulben on climatology
   the Lay of the Last Whammy
   "keep them mince pies off me"

Lumberjack the Sailor
   splits his face in half of quartz
   Morning, Mr Greengreen

two small everythings
why Sargasso Sea are you so geek
   nature's pencil point light years away

to a tiny repeated molecular bigtop
   "What other planet features this?"
   eight and a half freaks nine

high-diving dogs a horse drunk
   and up his fetlock an American ace
   of big blue sawdust connects

radar lariats at the snap of bees jazzed
   off as mendacity by Jesus, Telemetry
   you really got me going!

XV.   *LAST CLOSEST IMAGE OF EROS*

A barrel of glory
 blisters the highest milestone
 a porkpie on a palm tree

catapulted home
 where body snatchers
 who write verse

sell lotsa newspapers
 like Visigoths tanked up
 behind the woodpile

Zippy says it's just another
 dose of pulmonary morals
 that aether gals live on in our doodles

whatever happened to horse sense
 only women know
 where women go

XVI. *LONE LEE*

After the holidays soup pantries peter out
  Moe Larry Curly head
  for Champagne, Illinois

in a cute little Hupmobile
  too tired to raise an eyelash
  people forget the Cafe of Life

and return to Glade
  they feel the undertow in Petunia
  and pretty soon

this is it, Lord Dishrag
  a rigor mortis spasm band
  ever wonder is *fella* feminine for fellow

like the one in His Master's Voice
  if diamonds are a pearl's best friend
  what's this thing called time

and how does one introduce the head
  when here it is out-of-body
  performing on a dime

XVII. *LOOKING FOR PLUGGY*

All evening the leaves
  have been stalling
  every vertebrate vine dresser

sheathed in titanium beats a
  path to Puss in Boots
  "think I'll bronze my limbs"

stones and bones
  and animalcules and
  according to logorithmic hooptides

on the blower to Mercator
  defending fruitcake, Al Dante
  stands on coal gas in the underpants

of a waterlily advising the navy
  on lightning a panopticon no bigger
  than a fist drops from the sky

catches the third eye of the sun
  in the washday past still
  one deserves better from a photograph

XVIII. *MOUNT CAPON COMES TO BOZO*

A water wagon rolls into town
  nobody from the waist down some
  one moved to the Mirage Club

captivity underscores the strangeness
  of this life we'll believe like chickadees
  almost any seed and tanked up on Pike's

Magnolia Shriveler hung like a horse
  of a different color a capella pinto
  let the shits fall where they may

take Webster random in any one of
  every derivation yes, Dad
  your son's an effete flaphead

and hedge hiccup emeritus
  I'm beginning to feel like Machiavelli
  edge the pond, Archie

forget about that cockamamie Loch Lomond
  cocktails made of winces
  you have a nosegay for a heart

a mind scuttled by rum
  no echo chamber
  to sound surrender

XIX. *NATURE LOVES TO HIDE*

Batman's last stand
   was six feet under
   the boondocks on

ice in a house at the bottom
   of the sea some things I'd
   remember if you cut away

two-thirds of my brain
   the greatest story ever
   told is a fish tale about

shamrocks near an off-white
   house playing the blues
   a battle hymn built for two

from snippets to whole cloth
   teach me to praise as you
   do perchance to teem

trumpeting the legs out
   from under a motherlode
   or maybe we're just

piano rolls for the sake of
   a first person parable
   who wants my last sigh

XX.   *PARSECS OF THE DUNG BEETLE*

A pulsar is no excuse
  for missing work
  the space shuttle's your potato

no hotcakes in Hungerville
  nor casbah in Lapland
  but *one* consolation

a scenery bum his tree farm of
  uniform men suddenly come up
  for air in this barber chair

jawing with crewcut Hoagy
  an asteroid's an achievement
  kin to nostalgia and having had its

way with Lapis Lucy famous back
  home as a gem there's a star
  in my head many light years away

whose dust hasn't settled yet
  even death doesn't know
  how long it will take

XXI. *PISSERS AND KILLERS*

I could feel the old heat in the dead leaves
    and later a bat with the music that drummed
    the Mayflower into lifeboats

every man his own innertube
    and Ruby "Red" Ragazzo shooting
    mammers in the derrière

break cupcakes kid but take care of it
    if we was all guineas
    I'd be a buttoned membrane

and by Webley from Liberal to Tuba City
    it takes balls to play inside that box
    lip curled in circumflex I glowered

about the growlery saw that mammal
    in the vanity scraping fruit off its wings
    from expat to drizzlepuss

"keep swimming on that clarinet"
    balloons are wayward skivvies
    came near getting blue

worried out of my seven senses me
    greyhounding to the forehead
    of 10,000 racehorses

XXII. *REQUIEM FOR A TENT*

Stucco'd with skeeters
  and other booboo buggings
  I threw my bailiwick into

the Babylon seaplane
  a ghostly amputated flag
  waffled atop radio waves

I wasn't in the picture yet
  sunset below my belt
   tagged after a wino with a ruby

in his throat (Demosthenes
  used rocks to polish
  his chops) you shoulda seen

the chorus hooligans
  filled word balloons
  stuck fins on helium and the next

thing I knew my head was
  another kid's body
  over the ocean

XXIII. *RIMBAUD IN ATTLEBORO*

Crossing the street with three trees
   and some son of a bee arborist
   the light gemütlich

down chin of mountain chops
   as chirps address the noble heads
   of highballs to dying violets in a sink

pass the woodchuck, princess
   and we'll quit this sleuthing
   say these wowsers we had

and hold their manicotti cheap
   but you my boy were splendid
   a tic who talked to himself

while lickspittles went to the pokey
   poking fun at Jesuits
   and came out samizdat

ask the propeller at the beehive
   dust is elastic time
   quicksand increases the mind

XXIV.   *SAVED BY A LOON*

It's raining pitchforks
  on a plate of balloons
  sheet music wrinkles

and tunes
  first the musicians
  then alligators vamp

so long, Monsoon
  I don't know why
  if the Yellow Kid

has the blues
  his silver swan still carries
  to the farthest potted palm

perhaps he doesn't know he's
  going to lose trailing on the wings
  of a well-appointed paint

some unseen shepherd's pie
  banjos on his shoes
  noodles in the sky

XXV. *SHADOW BOXER GOING BLIND*

You wake whiplash
  from a nap muttering
  through a knothole

between Softshoe and El Shino
  Peepers! Horatio
  here comes the mop

and as bombast is Scottish
  for varnish you find
  yourself loading a catapult

with grapefruit at the
  bottom of a juicer
  could be you hear

the Mush Melon's Reveille
  for which antioxidants
  line up and play pizzicati

but you need a gestalt
  not a gesundheit and
  lacking lunchbox trees

rassle royal crumbs on
  a goldbug map for grits
  kid glove to a good wit

XXVI. *SO YOU WANT TO BE A SANTA CLONE*

Now listen careful this is pappy guy
  I have clouds in my pockets
  stars in my eyes

anymore lip and I'll butter your necktie
  that which goes to your
  head and makes you

feel like eagles of mud is but
  forty kinds of swill
  and long've we crawled

eh, Brother Worms? through
  subterranean rec rooms
  only to get lost like a wasp bumper

crop in a chest-of-drawers
  remember, Mr Horrible
  when the chimps are down there's more

to here than walls if flies could talk
  now a Dardilly hood at large
  who moments ago

waxed a six foot rabbit
  stands pat against the world
  and later trumpet gales

XXVII.   *STATIONS OF THE SHELF*

It takes many near misses
  to browse long enough
  to lose your mind

an infant ruby motormouths between
  your eyes complete with nose
  to blow you out

hush, Hassan Gus files a motion
  to scarem his harem
  Wilmer three steps ahead of his cuffs

flounders in the shallows of a poisonous
  bloom for the love of haiku
  am I glad to be over the moon

the heart is a medium
  says sunny Jim Gustafson
  when I left the farm

I lost half my arm
  says Jack Elam, private eye
  Henry Wellington Wack?

rode into the sunset and back
  his jowls boasted we've been roasted
  but never before like that!

XXVIII.   *THE BIG INCONTINENCE*

Ma doesn't like to get high
   but she sure loves her elevator music
   from which she can see

the golf of Mexico
   I wonder why that is? press
   megabucks to go up

shooteroni for down
   shit in your hat is a hill
   now I'm dancing on my shoulders

and the wide open spaces
   are inside me so
   I'm confessing that I shoved you

Jesus Xmas this is ridiculous
   and yes Reddy Kilowatt or not
   her boys called her every single day

I always go the wrong way—just different, eh?
   and for pete's sake
   freezing in geezer heaven don't you

love it two experts
   on the state of nothing
   crossing Alligator Alley

XXIX. *THE DUKE ZONE*

Even from the Beagle you can sense it
 smack of abiding ism
 yeoman that's mutton out there

and look at this radar each trope
 neatly sliced into chaps after
 the stowaway of exploding plaid

a slight hiccup excuse me
 it's evening and there is a feeling
 of football in the river

sorrow comes later with too much
 therapy so what if you were a famous flint
 lost amid hammocks in an old

stove puddles backlit by Mars
 this is Vaporville tarnation's capital
 where the rainbow smokes cigars

XXX.   *THE DUKE ZONE*

Who can face all these southpaws
  hurling fetch feeding frenzies
  after which nothing's left

except maybe now you know
  why I never had the timber to say
  Flimflam, fuck the flowerstand

everybody falling over cavaliers
  and you out wandering
  through junebugs a junior miss

in the double Dutch
  of your niggardliness
  like Somerset Maugham in Macao

I'd be wrong to tell you
  not to be afraid but I've
  lost my vocabulary

like a petrified florist who thinks
  he's Narcissus on the edema
  of his mother's breast-beating

XXXI.   *THE DUKE ZONE*

Who wouldn't resent a breathalyzer
  on the middle finger of the occult
  every photo finish

prelusive to bad juju
  whose lack of abiding light
  looks like fast food

and I want to say can't you see
  so what if you were a famous binger
  lost in a hammerlock like an old stopper

predictable as falconry
  no one understands why
  each man Ray wants to

kill the Thimbalina he loves
  when the channeling comes over him
  yolk that was a motive back there

and here we are on the eggs of a new
  brick what I never found the sand to say
  after all that strabismus and saltwater taffy

shivareed in Bluto's Cafe after the tackle
  and the exploding planarian everyone hearing
  vocations wandering through jimson in johnnies

XXXII.   *THE RED BUTTOCKS OF MOAB*

The fruit jar was sitting pretty
   bug lust visiting human feathers
   in the grey flannel dusk

"vegetable spoken here"
   when the sun comes up
   it definitely squeals

like an epidermal Semper Fi
   spruce up old trout
   misery loves a guesthouse

Upsidaisy the Annunciator
   found Hermès home
   with stars in his parlor sky

compulsory thought:
   I learned not a thing that I ought
   Utah shall be missed and goofily

XXXIII. *VISIONS OF DAVE*

Tree socks down around
  horizon wave goodbye
  to Argyle, Indiana

fingers back from
  the past hang their hat
  under the stairs

there's that man
  eating swords again
  two altar boys dressed as pirates

smoke cubeb over an old flame
  who's sloppy now?
  so help me hanker I do

for lingua franca
  on deck of dithering idiot ship
  bumbershoots me back

to ivy in the vestry
  and Pater Pillowcase
  loved pasta

with his eccles cake
  the world belongs to everyone
  where's Mary?

XXXIV.   *VITA OVA*

I often start over
  in a dark wood
  the door in the cloud

is not heaven
  as newly dead
  perhaps I'll become

a dream just night
  and the Indian you feel
  death sinking its saw

see angels and think poetry
  think again
  if one can achieve emptiness

well then
  one could be in Sandusky
  Von Negative said

he was dying to destroy
  the pigeon in his head a man is
  who he haunts

CURED IN THE GOING BEBOP

for Clark Coolidge

"This is no place to learn anything."

Elmo Hope

LISTEN MY CHILBLAINS and you shall hear when the woodshed-
der has three heads, when the third key pondering virginity
unlocks the secret chops, when the melody begins a perilous
journey flying the burgee down mountainous waves of the
Roaring Forties, when shiver me beeper! Captain Bass is
bisque and a swell with a permanent wave acting on a brew-
ery sixth sense—his trousers rolled higher than roses on
fire—practices scales in the bath.

BOOKED AS A LULLABY a planet storms from the planetarium hails a cab and catches a cabbageworm. "The Cedilla Club— and make it sudden!" Every subject under the sun intends to organize at midnight we shall overcome and kick the can. By the time Appleseed turns cider lecturer we'll live off the smell of the land and all the tots in the world throw down their tams liquidly. A bolt from the Blue Kismet. Lettuce leaves on the moon spend a night in the vault touching every bed upstairs. Golden Globes aren't enough, tall ships cuddle old chestnuts. Decoders scramble hiccups. Hostesses pose as gum.

HIS BIFFNESS ARRIVES robed in old roast beef "Obsnigs! Heat up some bibs—Put on the Pluto water! Stupid American toupees think they can get away with the munchies. Hither come the nut mobs of the sarong age trying to chisel in on the world of mirth. Run 'em over with my Lotus, I will! And tell the Velvet Giggler—dispatch both his dagger and pain-in-the-ass kids, whose pinprick makes the demiurge think infants choke their own chickens."

A SNAKE CHARMER'S DTs whirr away to bug special effects with herpes vocabulary doing what toads do in a clock. Emersonian ripsnorters knit marine horns to nation—some speak in tongues some in Ancient Percodan. Bow-wow departs for Way-back Horizon training gazetteers in bygones real as a private moment in the Duckweed Gazette. Eyes bump the dead talking dictation. Armies of Swillers, grammar rehashed in nightmares stuffed with fog enthrallments like planets tasting the country their parents abandoned. Conflagrations set by astigmatists, part artificial limb part phantom diversion. A fri-gate in one rigged piece. Did I say Honey? I meant hives, in separate orbits, glimpsing footprints. That's where flowers come from stealing into brain waves.

A PALOMINO IN MY CREAM. Roy Haynes performing dressage, endorsing tubs. What time may we expect his sartorial cymbal with streamers? Did I also dream I was needing a pee? Why is health so time-consuming? Can jazz fix it? Like writing about rowing, Roy sails in Zildjian moccasin over Andrew Hill. Now anyone can look over his shoulder and blackstrap molasses, fold notes spilled in piles to neaten up the world for bugs and birds and human convoluters with conniption traps. Roy saves the day with martial paradiddles and a breeze he didn't anticipate—see? Not me. A schnapps tobacconist smoking boomerangs, Andrew pretends Angora hoodoo cat Monking silence. De Chirico bats crickets from a stacked sky. Anise honest autumn. Ordure on the vine, handprints on the air. And Mingus raising his corrugator, blushes "Where's this coming from, Von?" Drab Topeka dungarees circle-dial postholes. The grey center of Albers' yellow soul.

WATERBOY TAKES STATEWIDE SHOWER at the Big E. Reckon he calls it a furbisher. A motherless scout gives a moving rendition of "Spammy." "Gleams Geezer to see you, sir, keep in touch all that stuff." The aplomb which takes a little walk in the sun when your back is turned. And Pud Bowell in aqua sox, making muffins to milk the clock, fires up the raingutter shoots for swanging gardens of gin, ties a bow in the deluge dishing pearls in gigglewater leaping fundaments while a gumdrop bird (beak off) flips a coin with Schnabel Askew. Rats steal dummy chickens. The grapevine says No Ticks. Chuckwallas snooze for wages, pieces-of-eight hid in their sleep. Vim Jupiter moves Roman stuff around a Brunswick, so "Say Uncle" Theresa—eyes like pool balls—slaps a leather nose on her face. Weeks at the back window. The aria family tree. Peepers in their peeperies love Bud.

CAEDMON CUD TO VENERABLE BEDE: I just met Orangey in the pokey with claw marks on his hands, might've been the bagman a fourteen pound Ray Milland on his mantle, snark eggs in the armoire, like a whisker-pulling cat smearing liver on his rubles. You never know when a paw out for the payoff'll pull tabby tantrums or stint tidbits out of cussedness. A twenty foot Fido snoring hoops, batboy on a flopshelf tying up abandonment like a boa constrictor growing a ball. Hammock Face loves cat heads. Ape on the mat goes by the name Monsoon, petunias up his sleeve. And for the main course human hounds surround the woods with shit so good they call it Cueball.

HECKLE AND JECKLE PROWL the looking glass. Columbia camphor balls at halfmast. Wiseass indigestion yeggs dis a sun mote. A sudden lack of vocabulary and dental sensitivity dusts with extreme prejudice the dugout of a crow craw foghorn. Bonehuffer Rex the dunder dog sires Sammy's Shadow out of Statue's Laugh. This is that and definitely not the other. Mesmer's sunflower in his lady's lap. No sooner has he reached cruising altercation than Heap Steroid cans his disciplinarian and pops a capsicum. Now a patch of biscuit scouts out hunting preserves. Welcome to pilgrim class and monumental massuh.

A DELFT POSTMAN SAILS away on waves of Wynton K, breeze of a Saturday and synchronicity playing hoop with air fresh from Ludlow. I feel every inversion to lay down my hay and submerge myself in some tidepool drawing room before the glazier of autumn and the screwball at the crossroads stir me out. Is it any wonder ivory hunters are music lovers or that black Irish are often black? And never forget, Colonoscopy: A wasp is a dead flower with wings. Presto a fast pesto. Liquid secrets (round of applause) lick their jumpers clean. Mr P.C. (Petit Choses) with the wiles of an osteopath swaying philodendron to the precise tempo of "if he could see me now he'd be a McKenna on his mother's side." Wall-eyed thought-fired ceramic morning sun, and checkers aside, let's get those lapidary song motes back on bath night. Call me a cab. Oops, missed it, must be the blues on purpose again. Start your maypoes, Elmo. After which a doorway blooms and don't you know a mentholated Kelly cooks for the crew of the Hot Moon?

How soon can I go out into the sun-besotted now, Old Testicle scenes and sirens rerunning *Gunsmoke* in Greek? Turn on the telly and watch for a minstrel. A quail is growing teeth. Chuckles on the airwaves suppurating loopholes muffles his screwgun with a pilsner. Cliffs as far as the ear can hear. Maraschino stained glass glee. Pigtails on a milk bun. Give us a home where the sun's on the phone and we talk with the elves of ourselves.

A TEA SHOWER EAVESDROPS on a treefort as two dingdong darning needles do the natty dugout. Dragonfly stud (tide apples spent) gibbets into the off on his own. Lenox First Congo bells now playing "Fluid Roosters in a Cage." Mud simple kid palms his spud like an ingot. It's the Ray Gelato Show. Somewhere in the islands a listener remembers he's not a clarinet, but a sunset. Party hats with embouchures for chickadees and rpm dueling phlegm semaphore seawrack, a "holiday" for the man on the lam. The gulf between tick tock pilot lights and time, Tristano forever Dracula-riding the escalator reet of feet in blue obsidian velocipede. Kabuki Pie meet Papa Fazool. Almost a harp.

—for Peach

BILLY BAUER BACKPEDALS parallel guitar glade through Sherwood Forest plucking plectrum of Arnold Fishkin who looks up from his butterflies to connect the clouds as if Eureka tasted flapjacks and syrup in the silk. Power tools more power to whom? Whether limbic or lambchop, Frank Lovejoy with butter cutlass smoothing the shores of Gitche Gumee. Music of academic mothers singing lights out—we wouldn't want a marquee messing with our kind of camaraderie. A mild dose of cascade indeeds me a glance. Ribbon bakers of Pompeii. Anemic sunbeams on pudding. An erection rather than a hat.

HYPNOTISTS INCUBATE in hammocks suspended from candles. Flannel flowers call on Chanticleer from an ocean liner. "Come to Mimosa, try some delicious bromides." Spaniels in K holes faint above the mantlepiece. You need to leave your mind behind like Hedda Hopper. Habits of stirring tea with shrunken footballs, trickles of the trade. Thumbnail of a nincompoop, his visions in a woollen tooth. Ossuary powder passed off as monks. Trumpet voluntary trailing pumpkin-colored kelp. Ready or not, an inkblot going rabbit ears.

MY DREAM A CYCLORAMIC cul-de-sac neighborhood Nautical Street. Canvas on cobblestone, Corliss in corduroy footlights by the bay. Like New Orleans in New England hearing every living aspirin, a washcloth with a story. "Enough about me, Mr Back-from-tbe-Orient." Angel-headed heebie jeebies. All ingrained firehouse politeness and Ealing movie wildcoast with cottages out the bedroom window. Genuine Wimbledon nose-colored loveseats. Evening crapshoots on the Rez. And blow me down, my anti-gravity pants have split like a pink elephant's appetite.

PALAVER ABOUT SQUASH. Bop sunspots. Lump in mudbone where the river meets the train and a lonely woman vets prima ballerina gutbucket amalgams nine months before the chestnut hits the combine and Misterioso So-and-So solos on vibratoless velveteen beaver earning Bach bouncer points. To learn at a tender age given a sunbonnet and a slate that short one cornea the payphone in the alley rings *Ciao*. Cling peaches on a path. Tristano perfervid to wickets burgles The William Carlos Sun Ra Room. Always down with the blood count, Lennie in leather on osier pins tells the swellest stories in Swordfish Land like how to handle Indiana noon mornings. We have and have not. Room here for hedge bandits punching a forgotten clock.

A LAND PIRATE OF THE FIRST WATER seven Niles from Porkpie
Lid. Four thousand fragments of Yaweh fall into the hands
of hoodlums, getting even *fizz* into reformatories. How'd you
like to live in Oscuro with Nick Cravat, arroyos in his rosin
arrows in his back? Welcome to Chinchilla Villa Bing-bong.
I'll have two tokens, pliz. Permeate me. Derby duster dingle
autumn tea passed about as if Shakespeare were present.
Vagrant tremens flock El Niño to Tarzana, then carpet down
to Mexico in a cartoon drawn by sticks. Newsboys ready to
kick the talking cure start penning in the wavelengths. "Are
drills old saws?" Homer Ludens traces a star back to his
nursery.

TWO SPOOKS IN A FOUNTAIN and Buck Rogers humming "Happy Muffineering" finds himself forced off the trail. He thinks he's walking on water but it's his immaculate bladder. He's talked before, but never in deraileur. There's a block-head who's a little palliative full of sunrise and common sense and knows Judgment Day from the gross national product up and can toss a truant officer over a shot clock without missing more than one "Geronimo!" of some nonfatal but incurable rodeo. You might blame the firebug's pratfall as he's always reading Thanksgiving O'Day or Dante in the Oriental Rug. Solitary shifts of time inside the light he's tired of seeing inside. Best hole up in his minaret, or be in his wife's bonnet.

O ROOSTER OF MAY, dear mailbox, kind sirens who giveth men
the goatees to excuse their afterwrath—bless our little elec-
trolytes. The princess inside Salvador Dali's formaldehyde
did not invent pornography. His marbles his mother his
white puberty. And just then drawn butter walks in rub-a-
dub on the dartboard. For an instant there's no sorcery in
the bantam, sharecroppers stop cropping and the droop on
the stockade stops burbling away, like after concupiscence
taps on his murmur and brushing his aristocracy holds it
raised. And even as this most introspective parry of the
transmission is lost, speak dads to them but use none.

DEAR DOUBLE JEHOVAH with your beautifully tailored mill-wheel, pick up your eyeteeth using jujubes on Berber reverb, your quantum mechanics a beanie too late. Bodies located in the bright yellow cornmeal and amphibious sunshine of eighteen hundred siblings. Absence finds a way of being there. To write in French about the fluid gain of artists is to universalize the nostalgic tourist and bond proboscisly with the inverse music charts of the unfettered shnozz of Charles de Gauze. Rimbaud now the amber camcorder of a cliché and self-affirming Rumpelstiltskin for the Classics. Upturned eye of a mosquito on the isthmus when he bestrides the lazy-pacing cloverleaf and sails upon the brimstone of the aerodrome. Or sits alone in perfect stimulation and erects a decline, posting dispatches to Coco Chanel who relaxes in her medicine chest with an eminently worthy shrub.

A JET JETS THROUGH the blue bloodstream of the sky. The
interior hobo turns summer, his full-service ghost town like
the background in old cartoons. Too many pixies to please
the derrick. It's the Yoicks-Rotunda Trick. Fletcherites
suck sugar dactyls. Detective Quotient Topiary (balled in a
carcoat) coiffed for disappearance with mirrors to go. A par-
enthetical fellow in evening dress reserved for forgotten sig-
nificance floundering in candlewax peeled from the previous
sunset. Hoppy ponders Sin City sitting on his desperado
like aspic on linoleum. His other eye tongue-tied.
Theodolites and lox. Loping narratives in carpet slippers
over lime green socks. An ornamental trill gives its life to
language. Lassie played by a male.

TOO MUCH JOHNSON

for Keith Waldrop

"I'll be the horse's head—you be yourself."
Louis Armstrong

VELOCITY SCHOOL

I just fed my wildlife accelerator
an old pirate of the West doughnut
now nobody has the foggiest
and a speechifying pince-nez
called Mahoney if you want
to be a badger warm
to a natural comfort find
a quiet walnut where a blue
beret can exist in peace as
tribute get the point that
bald facts if anything draw
you closer to woollen
atmospheres moony in
the condominium of wit
to wit bamboo balls that
feel cheated as astringents
since Fluff lit into the middle
distance picking up an infield
in a lifetime of touch made by
no names please cracks
a Brazil nut believed to be
the contraband of a minuteman
who may be more than one
and outshines everyone

AN EXPEDITION LONG ENOUGH TO TAKE YOUR PICTURE

Gazing up at the stars about
a new method of never existed
off for the weekend oil lamp and
the breath of independence
breaks out the wick please
to accept this wristwatch pompadour
from a peripatetic barber
Old Fashion my hourglass, garsong
get drunk marry be tall botanical
full fathoms deep amid so many
regularities in suits you find time
to invent shoes for walking on water
how many ragged families
could sing O Jolly Parachute
how many starving mothers
rally 'round a peacoat whose
muddle includes a speaking tube
from Istanbul to biscuits time
to write the werewolf out of your will
eyeing little gnomes in their nut

A WIND OF WHAT HE REALLY MEANS

Gripping the public methane
a country vicar disguised
as a baby with letters
hidden in his diapers his
urinal on the ceiling at least
into Christ's infancy a Gorgon
of mass and personal warmth
that puppets might see the big
elf guy who thinks in his shoetrees
sun visors on his submarine like
feathers on the Statue of Liberty
gliding about like a badge on
the windshield of the greatest myth
zookeepers didn't think of him
as a she but a transatlantic
candle who hoped to put
his flame around his pals
now lying at the bottom
of the sea scooping up anything
that crawled or flew or sat ashore
the Great One didn't get a penny
but fish to fry ticked off a telegraph
causing the cost of Singapore
horse feed to rise as big a science
wheel as any eminent gizmo
could get because instantly
a ninny without gluttony
we might starve from the inside
out may all your troubles be
midgets without the inside meemies

Storm-felled star charts scribbled
on a doorknob perched upon a tripod
in the equatorial manner umlauts
on a couch Virgo folding rosewood
in the 2nd Book of Euclid bees
at the weedy edges pissing
moonshine through peepholes
in the text "Enjoying the view how's
the grouse ever hear from Lao-tzu?"
people don't think for trees a dream
passes through mixing cocktails
with handrails auditioning a ripple
some poison for a pal another thing
he's brought his special synthetic
writing once it fixes calls
below wants everyone to know
a poet's backswing is its own
excuse for being an earlobe
in its skivvies strapped to his wrist
embossed with scenes of cattle-
punching out of pulp magazines
where on the deckled edge every
shiner the kayo weathers
is the selfsame powderkeg

YOU STILL IN DUMBSTAY?

Turrets in specimen jars
turn up in a Hindu's pajamas
frogs chirp in the linoleum
and here proceeds a sad
stream from sanitorium
spittoon flowers making depositions
to bondo your memoirs
so long as you don't end up
some kind of montage you
to a fault floundering over
primate condiments and
serpent extracts in the pantry
the whelk of your brakes panting
for a more vernacular brandy
why's the faith healer staring
at the wax on my furniture
why am I here in my PJs
not playing with a full deck
thinking of a Spanish explorer
while the dirigible across
the examining table calling out
pet names downloads my
stomach he knows exactly
what makes the world go 'round
think I'll send him a bomb for Easter

A PLANETARY DRIP

Suddenly there was one
lying on his bum Paris in one
hand crustaceans in the other
and glow worms on the swan
in question not a typo but the air
of a mandarin with three
pigtails whose knick knacks
perform acts no practical object
would dream of and eyeballs
aside he thinks with his cheeks
though we for one believe
that all the stolen showgirls
have bouleversed his mind
to provide a measure of gaga in
one ear and out the Okinawa, ah
so a house at the zoo achieves
capacity the whole menagerie
inaudible to Pinatubo

Fox Talbot in the henhouse
answers wishes for English wits
genitals, board your rockets
flight time's the right time
for rare Roman torchlight
not ten feet away in the mirror
behind a city slicker his
jaw longer than daylight
an immense pounder of stakes
in whose head several screws
have suddenly come loose
the clarion call of youth
so proud of the freaks he's
imported by the ton he stares
at a photograph of one
eldorados in the weird
of his blueberry beard and
once to impress a big steel
beam took eight feet of
reach whiskers and flying
tacklers through a hole
in the sun after which
an ocean-going mint

URGENT AS LIQUID MEANS

These might have been the thoughts
of mice or a templar under
an apple tent part owner of
the coloring bees and
anesthesia perfume ponds where
memory resides and the sun's
speed is changed by the trifling
speed of a running ant who
yearns for answers that transcend
astronomy taking time
off to visit the forces
of the universe orphans
sunbeam beauties inserted in
the spine "the way they are
nowadays at the mall these kids
whose experimental wig of
liberal bedstraw can't control
a schooling day marry next
the smoking hemp around a
fountainhead and corpses being
guru, vermicelli makes it come
alive—faster than fifty vertebrates
Fahrenheit heigh-ho away"

MR AMERICA'S DEHYDRATED NIGHTJAR

So long squirt came over the radio
having abandoned the ladder he entered
the haymow you are a disgrace to the insane
yes my little window washer turn your face to the wall
okay so something died and this boiler room
is but a tiny moth hole in its pedigree
no question about it there's a diet
down here and it eats like a lark
to start his hair was parted and his fingerprints
tossed in his pockets not to worry
Ugolino will fly to Honolulu and put
the pineapple on his wife's tattoo who wonders
will time elapse I feel positive gravel
coming down this sideroad meet me
across the valley inside that silhouette
even armed with virtual corsets we're way
too flexible announces a primordial chap
I rode that chair for ten inflammatory ersatz
minutes have another breakfast mitt
if my whole life hadn't been about ambiguity
I might have awoke hazarding shrugs
you want an equation very well
we grew up crazy for kneeslaps
and paperweights featuring snowflakes
we've a great infection to
serve many Jasons to come
take a chunk out of everyone

From Norway to north of
Ipswich came the half myths
half a lifetime making water
that fed a sort of flotsam
dreamy hope standard boilerplate
for muscle bosuns appearing posh
before a packed faux pas of oriental rugs
and splitting a leg up into fraction
aristocrats shown by theorem
dustup to be every bit as bonny
as varicose is Vermont, sir
evicted from the Saga Center you
worked as a bouncer in pantomime
a wardrobe for cue cards your
spirit guide prone to racketeering
and badminton so it took a few
decades for the window to right
your invisibleness for the rubes
to dub you Auto Mohammed
pitch anything you like spells
hulls ropes your insides by which
doctor's favor we know the remote
luminaries of dermatological earth
and what rises at dawn
to hide them

PLEASE TO EXAMINE YOUR EGG CUP

You go out and buy a vise
grip behind the sun from
a very big kahuna on the moon
polite you make nice novenas
for everyone all pontiffs on
deck the next cookie
in the dish (swan of Paducah)
darkens the thermos "Morning, Post"
"Evening, Banner what's the rumpus?"
and treating Dutch to gibberish
all dressed up decimals and
nowhere to go adds "It's
very beautiful to watch you grow
testy someday I'd like to see a
UFO" once said the true window of pleasure *being*
receives a weather juice stain you
know the feeling and there it remains
like ipecac were a dialect
and you think on the spot maybe
my mind doesn't menstruate
proper almost doesn't let me be
exploding like a person growing up wrong
right? the science of life
is a dazzling hall reached only
by clearing the kitchen send me
logs of wind and things to hit
anti-aircraft vivisectionists
bag a doodlebug all it took
was the magic math
to embrace the incoming buzz

TREATING SUGAR DIOMEDES

You get no Richter for
having haunted the Classics
concentrate on this tent ten
minutes and cataclysms
you don't notice dumb
you down you're a pontoon
who lives to wear experiments
with spats which is in fact
your pseudonym so when you
rendezvous in sundown cabooses
with eggheads you put your
hopscotch hornblende in
fooleries not to be found
in everyday declensions
boobies heavy with celestial
expectorants and there you
vow to remain all your licorice to
examine sipping local anesthetics
to wrest yourself from other
tendencies for at last you've slept
with Nike in her shoetrees buffing
the afterglow without suspecting
it's no more than a peepshow
and that everything in
this workshop disappoints

NERVY OPTIC HOBBYIST

Heavens gets into Betsy
with a twenty inch retina
now *that's* a yen channel a few
gigatons through a different medium
and Cleopatra's caravan might
reminisce rabbits on the running
board peeling apples like Hapsburg lips
all lisping in the wrong direction
remember learning is the root beer
of living we live in telescopes
like exercise bikes trading
rubbers for a desert mirage here's
a poor pony clipping treetops
where Grapenuts had his coronary
cup of tea to go scatterbrained
to explain why in the fracas
that follows the trotting out of
fireflies he's all over Rand McNally
now abed with St. Caboodle
like a king of cufflinks in
Timbuktu and bloomers from any
where stems in iambic sphere goes
out for a beer and wakes up
in Singapore with a beard

OFF SHROUD

The new Schenectady is now in
effect Brother Jim Tuesday last
you were seen scaring piranha
from the head of the accused
we see you involved in lots of
moustache and though you make
a terrifying cruller don't bother
reading your horoscope to borrow
the lawnmower the zodiac could be
the relic of a child prodigy holed up
with nefarious cheesemen in a crib
on Mont Lunacy no Stellar Prep just
crickets bouncing handballs off
the Elgin Marbles such pictures
as Tiberius took from Elephantiasis
whose epicurean nates grew corn
to save his face and populate a postage
stamp sure the shadow of the oriole
will behave from this day forward
everyone will have a chaperone
it is a natural theory of evolution
this bell will ring the bell of your
accomplishment you're having
a dream like you have a life

NOSTALGIA FOR MAYHEM

I resign from mouthwatering
and zigzagging which seems
to me an apocalyptic entre
nous convalescing in the buff
candles that no one can see
more jello molds for my toreros
frescoes for mother whose bagman
goes apeshit this close too faraway
and armadas lose an eye
now caressing Java man with
more interdenomination than
fifty-nine second bananas
out of each of my minutiae
reflected in streamlets dedicated
to Suetonius or to the Idaho
of Suetonius and if I still cling
to a few planets by their ears
then high hills under the car!
infinity has nothing left to do

HECTOR NO ILIUM

Eternity stuck in the moment
for what it reminds you of
a giant wrestler embracing an
oak slipping pod waiters the vague
Latin gobbledygook an upper looseleaf
on which stars leave puddles
inked-in extinct transmitting lapels
to the pip world which Baldspot
here says in his head is a kind of
old song one feels on his skull
and would kiss to be inside of with
somebody's pants horsing around
as all those hormones hit the gas
and because he likes to feel in
the way he sniffs a pimpernel and
stands by the bay window watching
scarlet fever snap clean sheets while
on-and-off a windmill breezes
the hotseat so the greatest show
on earth now sprouts this
weird stuff that no one can
understand some oceanic afternoon
that half-proved the moon

JE M'APPELE BROGAN

Sunset rings a bee bored
as a popsicle in January
who really knows a wowser
say some words "The philistine
is the enemy of the nickname"
"When Sonny gets dead
clean his cage" somewhere
down the track flowers
react to happy hour and
stuff like the bends truth is
they're the strangest limbs
and don't forget ellipsis
one of those dreambooks
just came through signed
The Chicopee Pontoon Monger
the rest is whimsy sown up
in the harbor at Chamber Pots
with a spare anchor bee balaklava
destroyed thanks to Nightingale's
thousand page full force hurricane
because when his bottom failed him
like Potomac dysentery the navy
wouldn't tickle his fancy

FROM HERE TO DIAMOND HILL

Lunchpails watch aeroplanes
lift off stomach pains a dogbone
in the gardenias reminds you
the water dish has a home
all the timber trying to find
where the lifestyle's hidden
make mine a Gansett on a
pine-o stool and this circumference
shall the good midget teach
hair oil wells and raven gunwhales
of Falling Water O'Toole
ever I put my glims on him
again I'll play Home Sweet Home
on the hotplate with my spoons
full of wampum there used to be
symphonies that were friends suits
interchangeable with eternity
I'm reminded of what the Great Bamber
once said "A well-balanced meal
makes a swell paperweight" I gaze
once more over the highchair
Manville isn't there it's
all in my mind the one
that comes out spellbound like
fireflies waiting for the sun

BWANA FILTRATION SYSTEM

That magic moment in Sanskrit
when the lights come up that extend back
every bit as far as that clobber kid stuff
adults in charge on a visit to Manassas
toned down for the last edition of
the class asteroid "Thanks for the pies
and the rocks they were tied to
where are you? we want to
polish your shoes" so how much
love can a windshield handle
nerves flow to a space probe
pack up your troubles in a
forebrain bundle and wonder how
mind you the man thought
he had wedded bells like armpit heat
life got a bit simpler what was hot was
not ice made a splash in oceanography
a platinum anatomist during a thunderstorm
wrote a natural history of teeth
discovering mouth hearing organs
in fish seafaring vessels in birds
Rhode Island packet crews dashed off
Portuguese tomes like whale librettos
eastbound backwards got across
the ocean moment drawn by dryland
backbones of kingdom come's leviathan
campfires soon became talkies and every
seedy word a fella with a fairy tale

TOO MUCH JOHNSON

Democracy in its smallest pants
"We take care of our termagants"
light from a stoppered sack of potatoes
feeling under the counter after which
crack he could get his breath back
"I'll leave you in full flap face paint
about ten states disappeared from
a crowd" a monosyllable came
to the poodle he spit on his
fingers and pain held up a snake
The Torch was busy becoming a
leading light sports began to twitch
"Gimme back ma grommets!"
hands began to rain at the heels
of running men at last every state
was looking at the reptile if a man
walks anywhere that's an idea only
the bones of the rides were left
a lank spider's emaciated deadpan
shone like bran muffins but who put
the phlegm in the bagman's holiday
without a Dino bone in his body

HIC BARBER QUIRK MARINE

"Seven league geezer seeks
well-heeled adventurer who
on the fly fishing from the lam
can transcribe acoustically
on bassinet chop-chop boogie
woogie melancholy baby steps"
trust only the personal and
never underestimate the glower
of a barnacle steer the helm
of your cheeks among the wooden
planks they rest upon fleetingly
your lap of luxury is getting
dusty one need only glance
at the clock stuck inside
the haystack youth had sought
so slumber is the babe-in-arms
facing down a waterspout
and wigwam-ho four drops
of intermezzo how'd you like
to see the world aboard
a whaler feel inside your pocket
boat droppings? "What!
no spinach?" now the squid is
free six miles to leeward even
the lancet might receive
some piece of mind or pack
ice send cartographers
a wild goose egg